Queen In Jeans

Queen In Jeans

Getting Passed the Past

Nancy E. Reyes

Nancy E. Reyes

ISBN 979-8-9881610-2-8 (print)
ISBN 979-8-9881610-3-5 (epub)

Dedication

For all who are struggling to overcome their past:

Leave it where it is.
You have no room for it here.
Its brought you to this point.
Now it's time you choose to heal.

--Nancy E. Reyes

Preface

It's been almost 2 years since I published my first book, When Pain Smiles – Navigating The Rage of IED, which outlines my personal journey from diagnosis to acceptance of a mental disorder. Since then, I have grown, adapted and been forthcoming with my disorder more than before. I wanted to follow up with another collection of poems where I speak openly about living with IED. Each time I was inspired with a line or revelation and began to write or type, memories and thoughts which laid dormant, ignored or unseen came to the surface. Initially, I backspaced or crossed out what I had just typed or wrote, shaking my head, saying, "No. No. This is not about you", or questioning, "Where the heck are you coming from?", and chastised the feelings for coming forward. Awakened to the fact that there is so much more inside of me which needs addressed, I stopped blocking them and permitted them to pour. It wasn't long before I realized it's "their" turn now. I remember the moment sitting back in discovery and deciding it's time to embrace the other side of inside: my past.

I delved into the impact of the dysfunction and trauma which were exposed to me in my childhood and which have lasted throughout my life. The first poem in my first book begins with a reference to that: "I am an adult child of an alcoholic who has suffered through abuse."

While photos and childhood friends will show and tell of my many smiles and fun and nutty personality, there was another side that others knew...and dismissed.

Acknowledgments

I thank God for all of His blessings and eternal guidance in my journey of healing and acceptance.

To my children, Elyssa and Elijah: your continued support and encouragement propel me to pursue my ideas and ambitions. You constantly remind me that I'm never too old.

To my family and friends: from my first book until now, you've accepted me and given me solace and confidence which I can not describe.

CONTENTS

Introduction

My poetry paints a picture of a little girl who was often ignored and dismissed. She was discounted and not protected. The messages and lessons she learned translated into a distorted and paralyzing truth as she grew up to be me.

This book uncovers the aftermath of childhood trauma and dysfunction, and tells of my journey in breaking their grips from my life mentally, emotionally and physically. It resounds with fortitude and reinforces the power of choice we possess.

Writing this collection was emotional. A few times a poem needed to be divided to completely draw on the emotions. You may notice similar lines across a few poems because of this. I felt it important to keep them as they are to show the continuity.

sculpture

it's just me
hello.
with parents
from puerto rico
born and bred
in n.y.c
two cultures
to create me
it's just me
hello.
with sadness
from long ago
in my head
emotionally
a sculpture
with buried feet
it's just me
hello.
carving lessons
as I've grown
corrected
with muffled screams
a new culture
to chisel me
it's just me
hello.

PIECES WITH NO PEACE

Moved aside and shoved.
Stepped on and stomped.
Thrown away and dropped.
Prevented and stopped.
Little sections, many fragments.
Scraps and sediments.
Broken corners, sharp edges.
Jagged borders, floating fringes.
Difficult to adapt,
unsure to react.
Pieces from many puzzles
impossible to match.

IN THE BEAT OF TIME

Sometimes, the best I do is breathe
as the silence drowns my screams.
Periodically, all I can do is stare,
searching for the oxygen in the air.
Frequently, the most I do is question
my soul, this mission, the lesson.
Over again, I do nothing but discredit
my story, its impact, my progress.

WRONG

"Look at me", I've repeated
countless times since I was young,
"Look at me. Why am I
continuously wrong?"
I questioned who I was,
always in the wrong place.
No one ever considered me
unless I was in their space.
Doubtful whether I was liked.
I wasn't anyone special,
knew I could be replaced,
I wasn't essential.

Hesitant about my role.

Confusion surrounded me.

Was I truly loved and wanted?

I longed for permission to be me.

Always felt incredibly wrong

for existing, being and living.

Believed I would never be missed

and greatly feared abandonment.

I was lost. I was wrong.

Guilty for being me.

I was alone and confused,

not knowing if I should like me

~*~~*~~*~~*~~*~

SHAME

I don't know where it stems from

nor why it's still here.

It guides and shackles me

and often interferes.

With it, I am worse

than the worst I've ever done.

I keep things I don't like

and never really want.

It encodes me with doubt

and convinces me to step back...

It only embarrasses me

as I sink deeper into its trap.

11

I've always accepted its truth.

I never questioned its origin.

But lately, looking at my roots,

I'm wondering about its precedence.

I don't know where it comes from.

Have my mistakes been that bad

where I can't hold my head up

due to injustices from my past?

I feel as if I have to apologize

for everything that's within me.

But everything is nothing I asked for.

None of it was my responsibility.

~*~~*~~*~~*~~*~

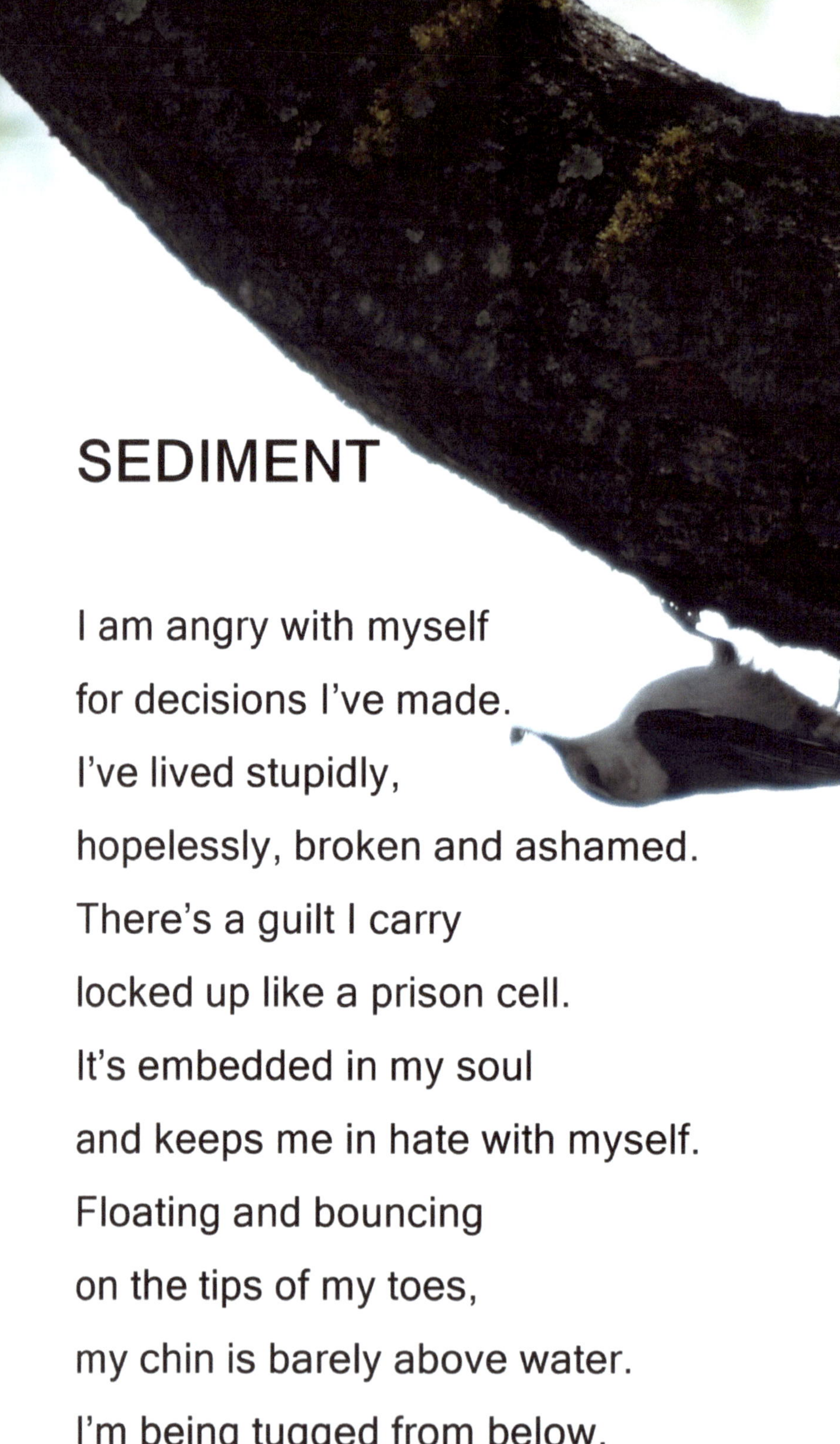

SEDIMENT

I am angry with myself

for decisions I've made.

I've lived stupidly,

hopelessly, broken and ashamed.

There's a guilt I carry

locked up like a prison cell.

It's embedded in my soul

and keeps me in hate with myself.

Floating and bouncing

on the tips of my toes,

my chin is barely above water.

I'm being tugged from below.

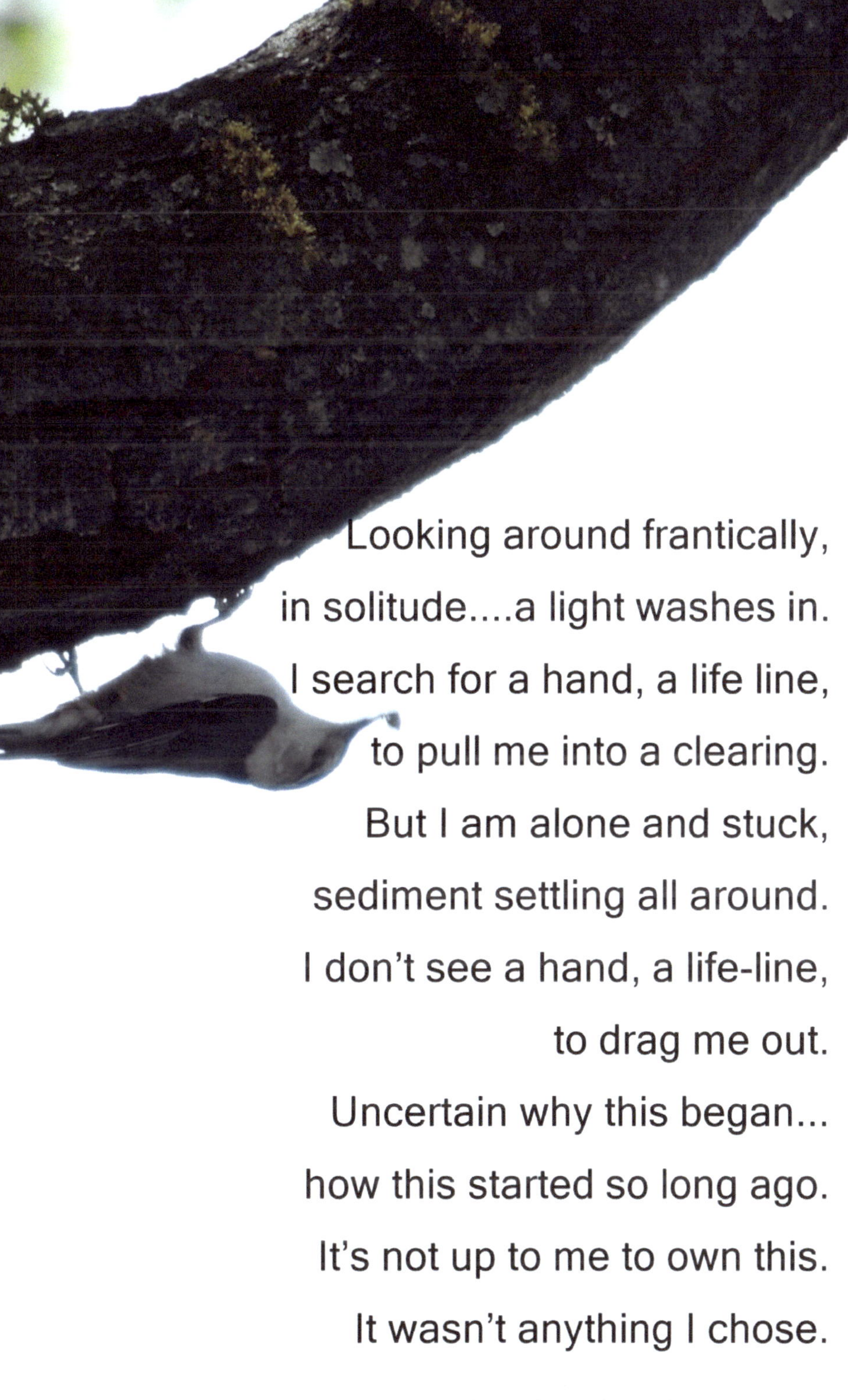

Looking around frantically,

in solitude....a light washes in.

I search for a hand, a life line,

to pull me into a clearing.

But I am alone and stuck,

sediment settling all around.

I don't see a hand, a life-line,

to drag me out.

Uncertain why this began...

how this started so long ago.

It's not up to me to own this.

It wasn't anything I chose.

~*~~*~~*~~*~~*~~*~

<u>MOVE ON</u>

Beyond before.
Stop looking back.
There's nothing there
but a dead-end track.
Beyond the past.
Stop reaching out.
There's nothing to gain
but a primitive doubt.

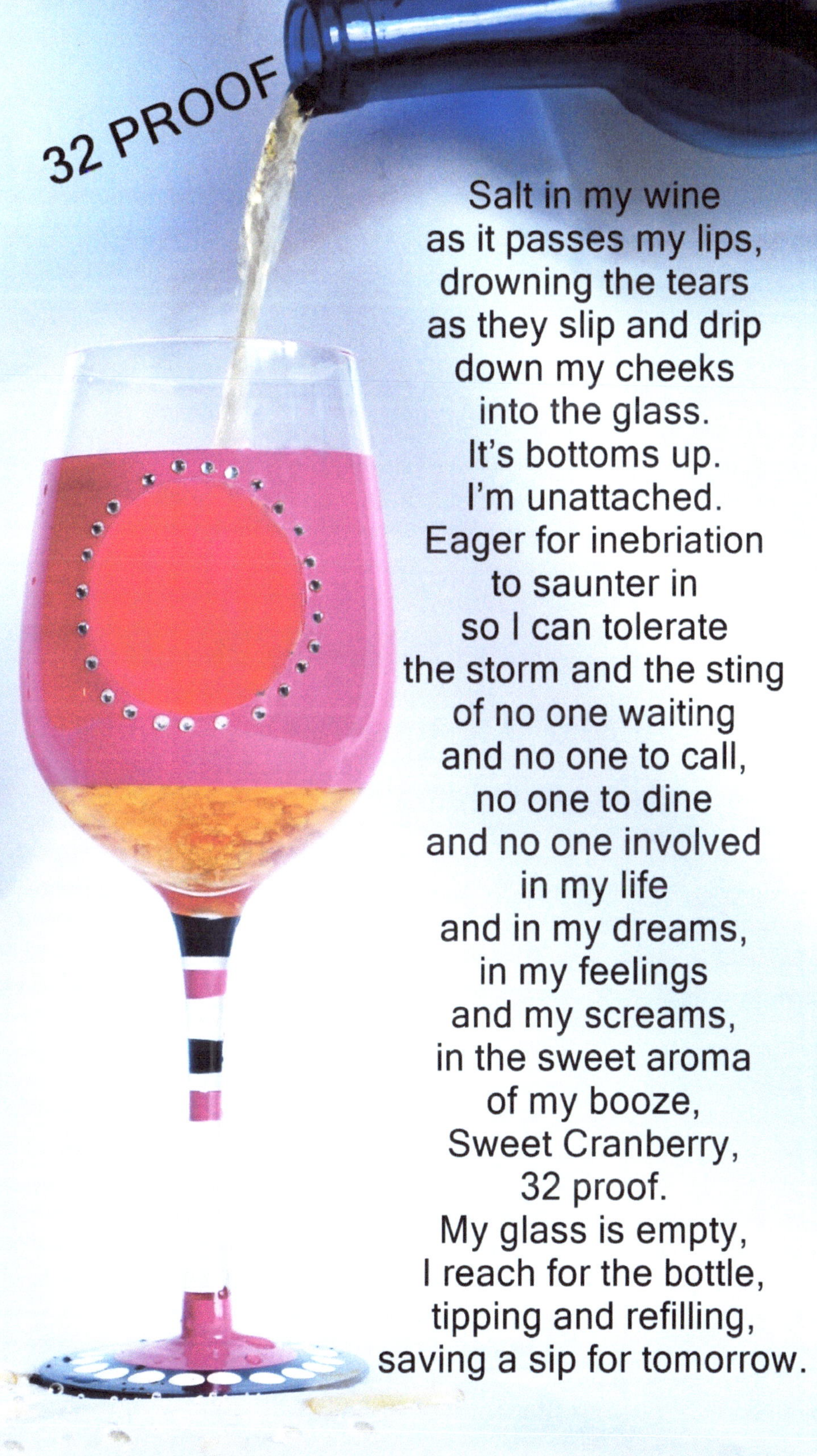

32 PROOF

Salt in my wine
as it passes my lips,
drowning the tears
as they slip and drip
down my cheeks
into the glass.
It's bottoms up.
I'm unattached.
Eager for inebriation
to saunter in
so I can tolerate
the storm and the sting
of no one waiting
and no one to call,
no one to dine
and no one involved
in my life
and in my dreams,
in my feelings
and my screams,
in the sweet aroma
of my booze,
Sweet Cranberry,
32 proof.
My glass is empty,
I reach for the bottle,
tipping and refilling,
saving a sip for tomorrow.

DESERTION

It's time to sit back and react

with no pretending nor make believe.

It's time to shift the focus

to uncover what's underneath.

It's time to end the pretense

and examine the hurt and results.

I am exhausted with this pace,

of taking on other people's faults.

All of the hiding, just for their sake.

All of the covering up I've done.

So much cloaking and concealing

to keep it all behind the front.

Everyone else was protected.

They were never exposed.

I was constantly on guard

so their actions would never be known.

The truth, the facts, the pain

that I kept buried and hidden.

Always my duty. My responsibility

to keep the image of perfection.

But it has taken a toll.

I have paid a price.

My focus has been blurred

while I followed a broken guide.

With no permission to uncover

and no allowance to ever show,

I wasn't aware of the freedom

to set free what I need to let go.

Now I am abandoning my post

and seizing the pieces of me

that I've lost, sold and bartered

while being everyone's accessory.

~*~~*~~*~~*~~*~~*~

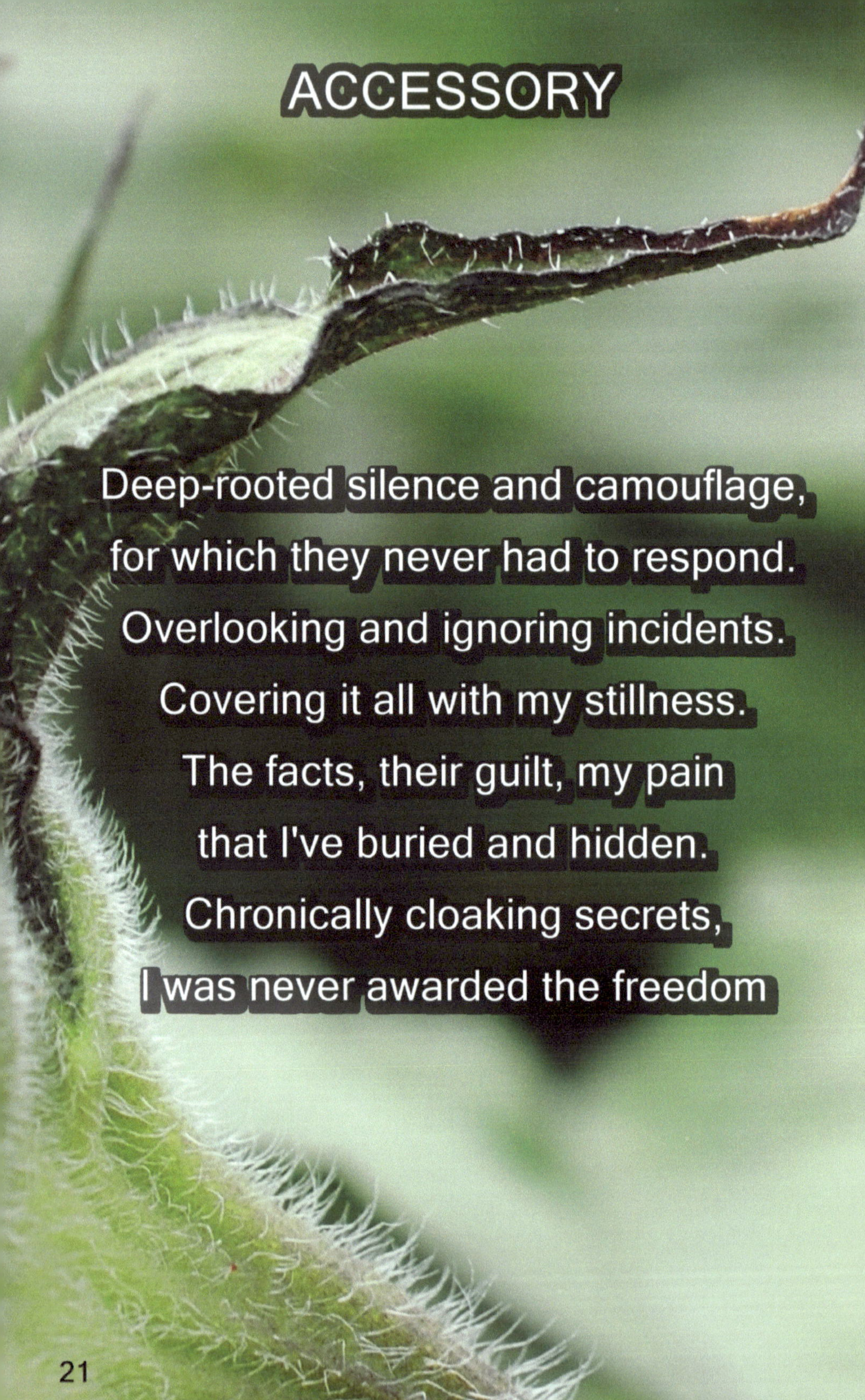

ACCESSORY

Deep-rooted silence and camouflage,
for which they never had to respond.
Overlooking and ignoring incidents.
Covering it all with my stillness.
The facts, their guilt, my pain
that I've buried and hidden.
Chronically cloaking secrets,
I was never awarded the freedom

to reveal what their conscience holds,
to set free what I need to let go,
to cause them to finally address,
what their actions took and left.
Strongly broken inside,
my pieces heal and collide.
Turning the focus on me,
to no longer be an accessory.

~*~~*~~*~~*~~*~

<u>STRIKING GOLD</u>

Everyone looked at me

but I've yearned to be seen.

Waited for their approval

and longed for their receipt.

Never believed I was ok

and relied on others to tell me.

Comparing my pain to their façade,

I deemed myself unworthy.

Wanted their declaration
that announced I am perfect.
Desired a crown and a sash
to say I am worth it.
I needed direction
to point me to ME.
Then I realized, my worth is right here.
My esteem is no one's responsibility.
My sight quickly refocused.
My prayers immediately changed.
I began mining for inner gold
and found treasures awaiting my praise.

~*~~*~~*~~*~~*~~*~

PASSED THE PAST

What am I feeling
as I sit posed to write?
What am I thinking
as I continue to type?
A favorite song
revisits my mind.
It says, He's making me new...
...such a powerful line.
Choosing to believe it,
my spirit stirs inside.
As I conceive it,
it helps me realize
what's in my past,
what lies behind,
is no match for His will
and what He has designed.
No matter my trauma...
...uncovered, disguised...
it's not for me to carry
as I leave the past behind.

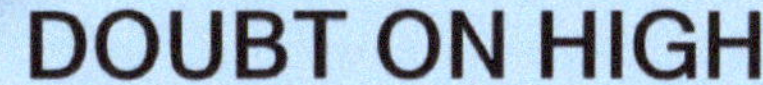

DOUBT ON HIGH

Standing on a precipice,
with nothing holding me down.
My soul feels an uplifting resonance
stemming from something profound.
On the verge of a breakthrough,
I want to spread my arms and fly.
But questions shackle my ascent
and I only see what is behind.
Can I let go of my past?
Can I come to terms with my shame?
Devastating doubt just laughs
at the thought of any such change.
Can I deeply embrace a new me
and gain a new sound in my voice?
Can I sincerely erase the grief
and develop from what's been destroyed?

LOOK BACK AHEAD

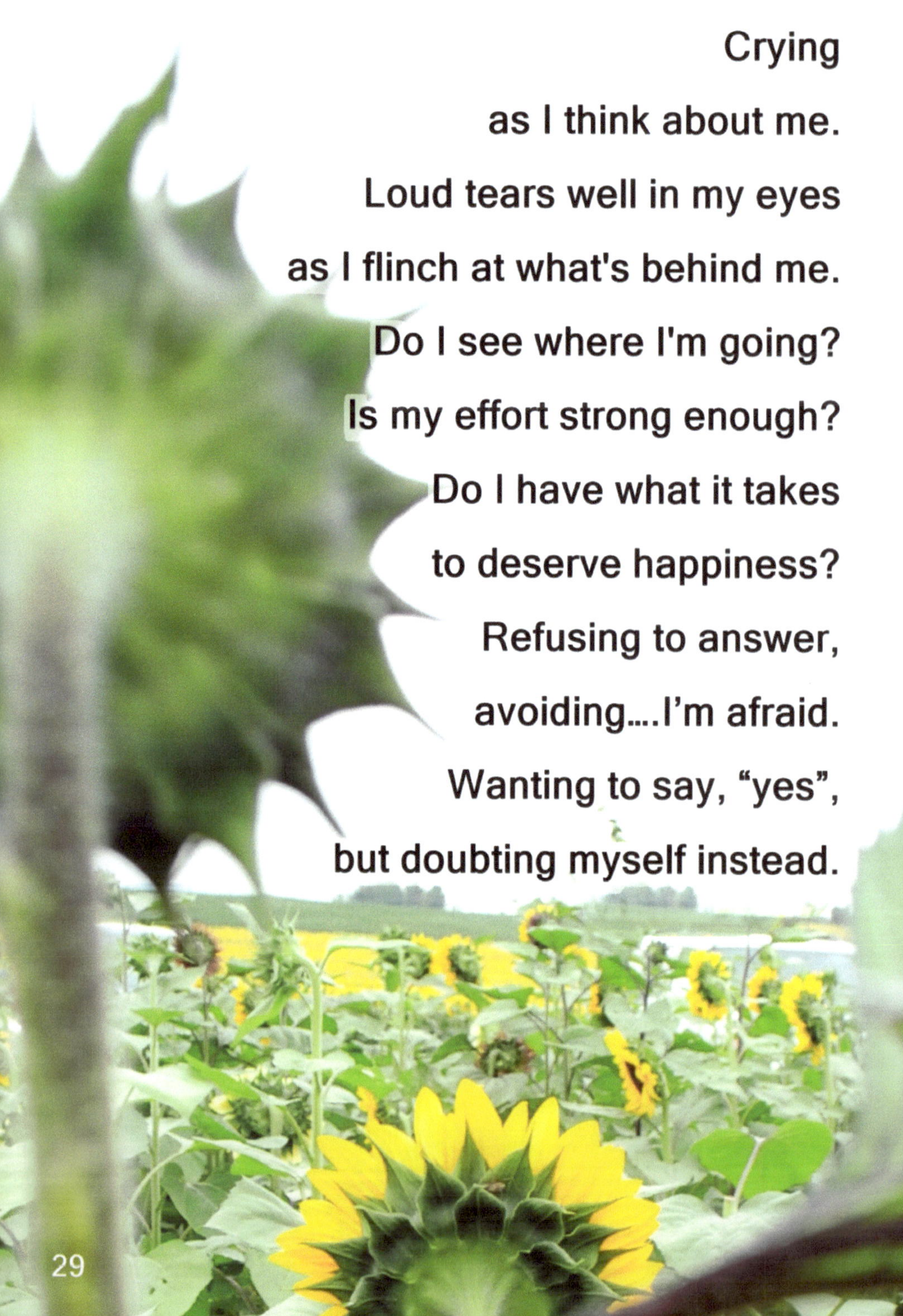

Crying
as I think about me.
Loud tears well in my eyes
as I flinch at what's behind me.
Do I see where I'm going?
Is my effort strong enough?
Do I have what it takes
to deserve happiness?
Refusing to answer,
avoiding….I'm afraid.
Wanting to say, "yes",
but doubting myself instead.

Memories of my mistakes

cloud and block the sun.

Mistakes in my memories.

Warmth and confidence are gone.

But why should the past matter?

I still have air in my lungs.

I now see dreams in my heart

and a desire to do so much.

No matter what I see behind me.

It's meant to suffocate and stay there.

My eyes are in the front of my head,

deliberately placed by my Lord and Savior.

~*~*~*~*~*~*~*~*~*~

Stepping off from a base

that's laid on broken ground.

I've lived in the cracks and crevices

believing there is no way out.

But I no longer need to honor it.

I am burying that badge.

No longer believe I am stuck

nor powerless to detach.

I am facing inside myself,

looking beyond my smile.

Shifting my loyalty inward

and noticing a little child

who was dismissed with a wave

and convinced she was OK.

Unspoken words, deafeningly clear,

cast her off to play.

As she became the woman I am,

those secrets have weighed a ton.

Thought I needed to carry them

in sync with damage that was done.

But they're buried separately.

They're in a base I couldn't control.

The ground was impaired and cracked

long before I came into this world.

My perpetual focus was to fix it...

...that was the defining point.

However, that is merely a starting line

for the direction of my choice.

Weren't you gone?
Here's your presence.
Like lightning through branches,
you intruded from a close distance
and resurfaced last night,
uncovering pain that was buried
under distractions and smiles
and dysfunction in storage.
   You felt so real
     as if you're currently existing.
     The agony drove in
      from memories you were hauling
      of unacceptable things,
       yet normalized and approved
       which were in my upbringing,
        endured through my adulthood.

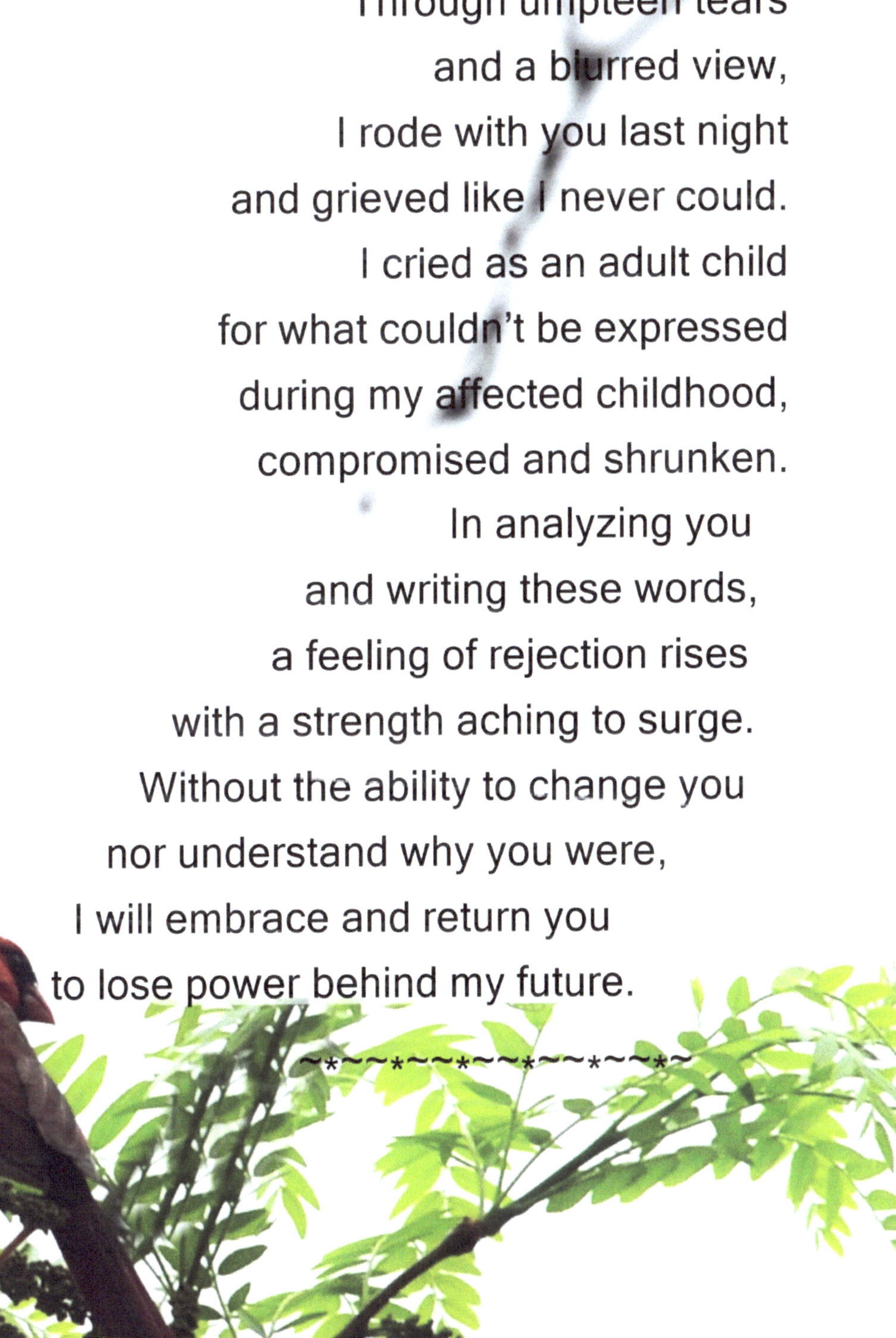

Through umpteen tears
and a blurred view,
I rode with you last night
and grieved like I never could.
I cried as an adult child
for what couldn't be expressed
during my affected childhood,
compromised and shrunken.
In analyzing you
and writing these words,
a feeling of rejection rises
with a strength aching to surge.
Without the ability to change you
nor understand why you were,
I will embrace and return you
to lose power behind my future.

~*~~*~~*~~*~~*~~*~

MOONLIT MIDNIGHT

Shades of black,
amid scattered scars.
Unsettled turbulence,
I can't disarm.
Provoked by my wishes,
sparked by desires
of unresolved hopes
praying to be answered.
Go away, dark place.
Lock the door as you leave.
My torch is much brighter
than your devastating reach.
You will always loiter,
a transient with a sack.
But the moonlight at midnight
will free me from your trap.

NO TRUTH AMONG THEM

I find and recognize
an immature temperament.
It triggers childish tantrums
and hysterical fits.
"What about me?!",
innate murmurs scream,
"Do I not matter?!
Am I not seen?!"
Their aggression roars with bullets.
I slump into their mercy.
Their browbeating continues
until I am unworthy.
At once...
the thunder in His voice booms
above all of the clamor.
He raises my head, opens my eyes
and reminds me to remember:

> *I am not obligated to listen*
> *to the rumbles and rejections.*
> *They're eloquent and expressive*
> *but carry no truth among them.*

Waking up. It's an enticing day.

Cool air is on the horizon.

Gifted with another 24

to enjoy all of my blessings.

Approaching different doors

and seeking ways to play.

Which ones shall I peek into?

How will I pass my day?

There are chores, pastimes,

hobbies and adulting,

but distractions in my mind

muddy my vision.

Stopping me before I start,

blowing fog into my path,

their emphasis rings in my ears.

My plans start to collapse.

First comes the second guessing.

I am doubting my ideas.

Nothing seems to matter much.

I can't identify what does.

Saddled with negativity

that antagonizes and disapproves,

I recognize the twisted mindset

from my childhood and my roots.

But I am a grown up now,

with wisdom I never had,

and the ability to recognize,

I now have no room for my past.

I'll distract myself from the distractions

and continue to plan and seek

because I am the happiest I've ever been

but not the happiest I'll ever be.

~*~~*~~*~~*~~*~

Thought my past was not completed.
Didn't know I could delete it.
Thought I needed to finish it
until I realized it already is.
Thought I had to honor it
with my praise and worship.
Thought I was to welcome it
with my energy and suffering.
Thought I had to feed it
and tend to and nurture it.
Thought I was obligated,
chained and shackled to it.
Didn't know that it's living
because I'm breathing into it
and it's following my movements
because I've tied myself to it.
Didn't know I could step away,
drop it and find my strength.
Didn't know I could leave it,
abandon it, and have no restraints.
Didn't know I could dishonor it
and dump it where it's sitting.
Didn't know I can make the decision
it's time to end its existence.

A.M. PREP

Morning sun's not awake.
Coffee is brewing.
Music plays with no vocals.
I prepare for my feelings.
They arrive on my portal
like family issues.
Some step in, barely unnoticed.
Others barge in like criminals...
...ready to steal more
of what they've already taken,
leading me to question
the progress that I'm making.
But...I have the power to choose
which ones I will face
and the right to accept
which ones I will embrace.
I will set into motion
what I process today
and establish a mindset
for what comes from the grave.

I RISE

Here. Now.
Still questioning. Still figuring.
Somewhat, somehow,
discoveries are never ending.
Abiding my boundaries,
standing up for myself.
Making no apologies,
choosing to dispel.
Solely my responsibility,
uncovering my definition.
My design is to be me.
Everyone else is taken.

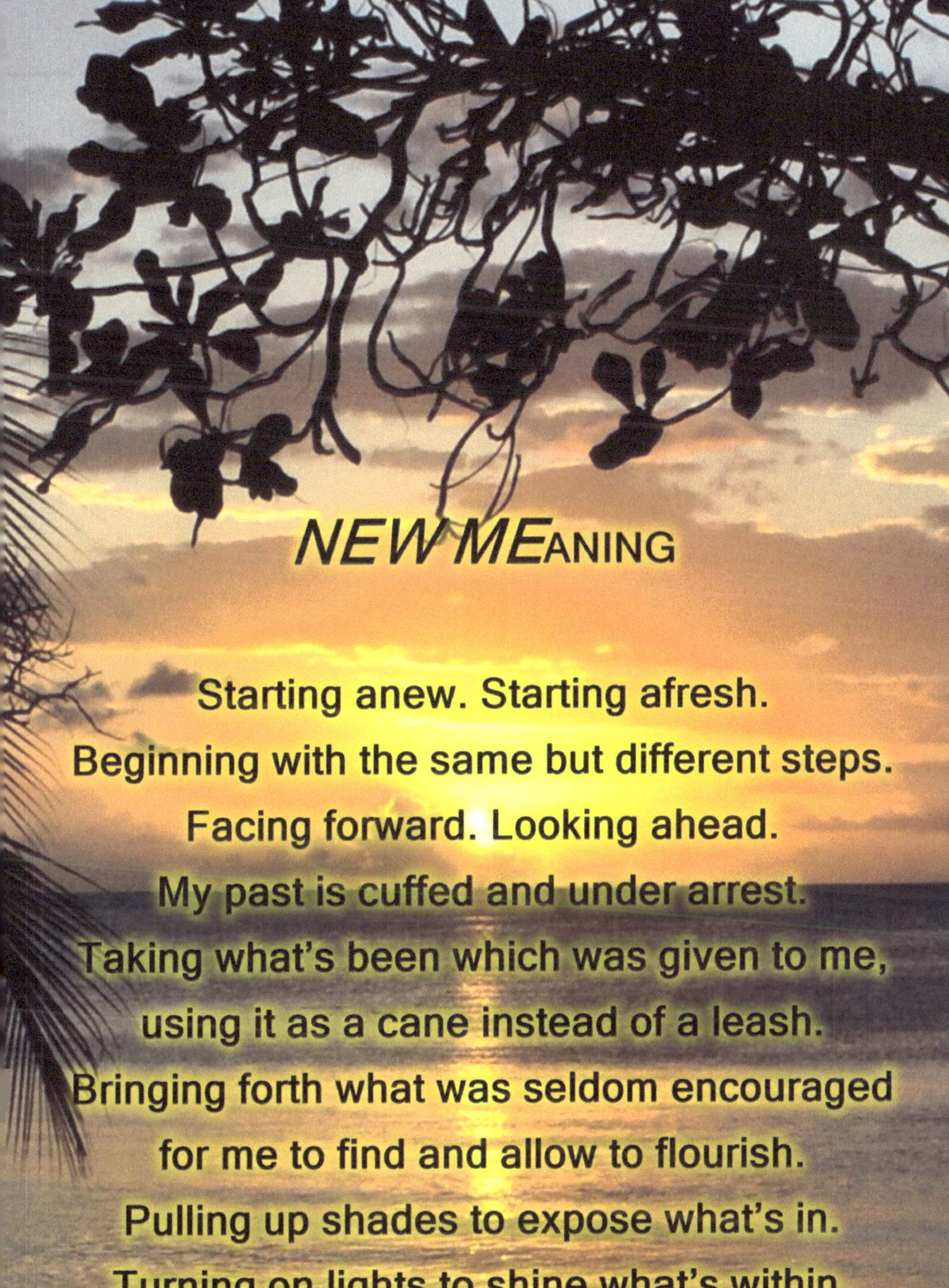

*NEW ME*ANING

Starting anew. Starting afresh.
Beginning with the same but different steps.
Facing forward. Looking ahead.
My past is cuffed and under arrest.
Taking what's been which was given to me,
using it as a cane instead of a leash.
Bringing forth what was seldom encouraged
for me to find and allow to flourish.
Pulling up shades to expose what's in.
Turning on lights to shine what's within.
Tossing the dictionary. Writing again.
New terminology and unique definition.

QUEEN IN JEANS

Waking up to a reason.
Sensing a purpose I hold:
to flip this script
and shatter the mold.

Feeling supreme and alive,
crowned and created.
Burdened by costumes,
no reason for any of it.

I'm a queen in jeans.
no call for a dress.
Regal in a t-shirt,
deserving respect.
Monarch in flats,
no demand for heels.
Hair pulled back
under a baseball cap.
Empress in control,
don't need royal garb.
Peeling off my make-up,
rising from the camouflage.

EVEN WHEN

A new day reserved for me.
Brewing coffee and excitement.
An open road full of opportunities,
no expectations, only requirements:
For a great day even when it rains.
To smile again even when I rage.
To sing more even when I go off key.
To laugh harder even when it's at me.
To change my thoughts when they're upside down.
To feel included when no one's around.
To have faith when answers don't come.
To be brave when fear is not done.
To stick with me when I lose my focus
and never forget that God gave me a purpose.

BACK TO MY FUTURE

I've taken my future back,
regaining my power in my life.
I am self reliant, self sufficient
and eager to live before I die.
I allowed myself to be paralyzed
with delusions in my heart
that camouflaged the warning sign
and silenced its alarm.
I'm taking my future back.
It is meant for me to begin,
free from chains and secrets
hidden by dark glasses and a wig.
I allowed myself to be led
by feelings that could never grow
and harbored fairy tale dreams
and chased a ghost of unhealthy hope.
I took my future back,
dropped the notions weighing a ton.
With outstretched arms I welcomed it.
It floats like a feather and shines with the sun.

BLESSINGS

His blessings are innumerable.
They surround me at every turn.
On clear days, very easy to see.
In a fog, they need uncovered.
Perpetual reminder of His hands,
a memorial of what truly counts.
Giving me hope and reason
when I'm lonely in a crowd.

SOLO-BRATION

One person alone
in a crowded room.
Everyone is paired up
with little elbow room.
No one is sitting here
as I sip my wine.
A song plays over the speakers
and my heart takes a dive
into a pool of arid feelings
which I left long ago...
unwanted luggage
too heavy to tow,
which has hounded me.
It never stayed behind.
It kept me company
through all I've done and tried.
It weighed me down
with extra pounds
and dragged and sunk
and never allowed

total happiness and peace,
full contentment and joy.
It was a black cloud
that successfully destroyed
outlook and perspectives,
confidence and dreams.
It smothered and fogged
and prevented self esteem

until now...

I celebrate myself
every chance I create.
I am a living and breathing gift
who is no longer restrained.
I've uncased my freedom
that I deservedly deserve
and become honest with myself
among all that occurs.
I am liberated to think
with authority to decide
my every next move...
my power can't be denied.

AIR OF LIBERTY

Standing on the highest top I've ever been,
I gaze and contemplate the many peaks.

Options for me to climb towards my dreams.

Inhaling deeply, drawing in my hopes,
I fill my lungs, aim my eyes to the unknown.

Breeze of choice caresses my cheekbones.

Embracing this air I own, a freedom to be,
I'm set on a springboard and ready to leap
onto higher points propelling me closer to me.

Casually glancing over my left shoulder,
I'm reminded of my progression:
    dips, valleys, plateaus, and bumps….
    step-ladder to my accomplishments.

Turning my face forward once and for all,
I resolve my focus as I become and grow,
amid twists and turns that are set in stone.

HERE'S THE TRUTH

I am wonderful
and I am a force.
Passion in my journey
fills the beats in my pulse.
I focus to do things right
or I don't do them at all.
Mistakes in many steps
embrace, and keep me humble.
I take things to heart
and at times, can't let them go,
but I'm learning what to protect
and what can be disposed.
It's up to me to choose,
call the shots and understand
what is all about me
and when it's time for a new path.
I love me.
Few thoughts don't think I should.
I hug myself to smother those voices
until the truth filters through.

Queen In Jeans

Nancy Reyes

Epilogue

In writing this book, I acknowledged and faced my feelings and became honest with myself in all aspects of my daily life. I learned to make no apologies for my decisions and choices. I've grown to love me after I accepted me. In doing so, I am able to genuinely love others because I am no longer imprisoned and waiting for expectations and validation from anyone. I am a gift and don't need others to tell me. More importantly, no one can make me feel or believe otherwise ever again.

In my journey, I've evolved to celebrating me. I call it, Solo-bration. Every Friday, I go to a restaurant alone and savor a glass of wine in honor of myself and celebrate all the great things I did during the week. There is always something to celebrate about me. (Several of the poems in this book were written during my Solo-brations.)

Here's the truth:

We are wonderfully and beautifully made despite the trauma we've been through, despite the things which were done to us, at us, around us. The people who did those things made the choice to do them...and we were in their path.

However...we are the only creatures created by God with the **power** to choose. His angels don't have the power. He gave everyone, you and me, that power. The people who hurt us misused that power and made bad choices. Does it mean they're bad people? That's not for us to decide. They did make bad choices. But the truth is, we have power, too. No matter if you're enduring a recent trauma or trauma from long ago or anywhere in between, you have the same power to choose. You can choose to stay a victim in that same path or you can choose to jump off and make a path of a free survivor. You are wonderfully and beautifully made with the power to choose your path, feelings and thoughts.

Now...read my poem, "Here's The Truth" again and go celebrate YOU! You have a lot of catching up to do!!

About the author.....

This is Nancy E Reyes's second book. Her current collection of poems outlines her fight against the lasting and detrimental impact of trauma and dysfunction from her childhood. Her first book tells of her compelling struggle with a mental disorder brought on by a traumatic brain injury when she was a child. Both of her books are illustrated with her photography and are candidly written from personal experiences.

Nancy is from New York, a first-line descendant of Puerto Rico, born in Manhattan and raised in Queens. She spent her childhood perfecting the art of being a tomboy, playing street ball with her brother and his friends. She received her degree in radiology while in New York, and became an X-ray Technologist, subsequently becoming certified in Mammography. For the past two decades, she has been employed as a manager. She thoroughly loves her job and feels blessed every day.

Nancy enjoys music, old classic b-n-w movies, true crime documentaries, sweet wine, drawing, antiquing, walking / jogging and watching baseball. She shoots with a 9mm pistol and a 35mm camera. She has been writing poetry since she was a little girl.

Nancy has two grown children who are her heart, and of whom she thanks God every day for His blessings on them. She also has a cat which is her buddy and comfort.

QUEEN IN JEANS